# AFRICAN POETRY

# AFRICAN POETRY

*An anthology of traditional African poems*

COMPILED AND EDITED BY
ULLI BEIER

ILLUSTRATED BY
SUSANNE WENGER

CAMBRIDGE
AT THE UNIVERSITY PRESS
1966

PUBLISHED BY

THE SYNDICS OF THE CAMBRIDGE UNIVERSITY PRESS

Bentley House, 200 Euston Road, London N.W.1
American Branch: 32 East 57th Street, New York, N.Y. 10022
West African Office: P.M.B. 5181, Ibadan, Nigeria

THIS SELECTION

©

CAMBRIDGE UNIVERSITY PRESS

1966

Printed in Great Britain at the University Printing House, Cambridge
(Brooke Crutchley, University Printer)

LIBRARY OF CONGRESS CATALOGUE
CARD NUMBER: 66-12750

# CONTENTS

7

# PREFACE

It would seem natural to use traditional African poetry as part of the introduction to poetry in African schools and universities. Unfortunately it is hard to come by. While there are many volumes of collected folk-tales and fables on the market, it is difficult to lay hands on collections of traditional poetry. Most translations of African poetry have been made by anthropologists, who were naturally more interested in the religious or sociological significance of the poems than in their literary merit. Many of these translations are quite unsuitable for school reading. Those translations that come across as literature are scattered in numerous volumes, many of them out of print, and most of them not in English. An attempt has been made here to put together some of the available material to serve as a school reader in poetry.

It is inevitable that these poems have lost a great deal in translation. The music of an African language can never be put into English. No European language can imitate the sound effects of a tonal language. Moreover, many of the subtleties of the rhythm have been lost. Yet some of the translations at least give an intimation of the intricate rhythms of African poetry: Leon Damas's translation of *Glory to Moshesh* comes to mind and Miriam Koshland's of *Hymn to Lightning*.

I should like to thank all the collectors and translators for allowing me to use their poems in this volume and I should like to express my debt in particular to Eckart von Sydow whose anthology *Dichtungen der Naturvölker* has served as an inspiration to this volume and on whose pioneering work I have drawn heavily.

*Oshogbo*                                                    ULLI BEIER
*May 1964*

# INTRODUCTION

Poetry has occupied a central place in the life of traditional
African societies. Praise-singers, drummers, priests, hunters,
masqueraders—they all had to recite and invent poetry. The
family rites connected with birth, marriage or death, the
installations of chiefs or religious festivals alike were all
occasions for the recitation of poetry. Equally important is
perhaps the poetry of everyday life: the young girl pounding
yam sings about her lover, the hunter on his way to the
forest sings in praise of the animals he is going to hunt. In
the absence of written language, everybody becomes a bit of
a poet himself. Nothing is absolutely fixed, or determined,
and everybody is free to add new lines to known songs and
poems to suit his own circumstances. Traditional African
societies have always had their professional poets, of course,
but they are not set apart from the community in the way the
modern European poet is. They have not lived in isolation,
composing for only a handful of people. Their creations
become common property immediately. Others take them
up, change and modify them: nobody claims authorship.

The poems in this book come from widely different tribes
and cultures, including the Yoruba and Ewe of West Africa,
the Zulu and Bushmen of South Africa, the Galla and Swahili
of East Africa, and even the ancient Egyptians—whose are the
only poems in this volume that were handed down in a written
form. The themes of these poems are the great familiar

themes of all poetry. The Yoruba poet praises Almighty God as the Eternal One:

> Young ones never hear the death of cloth
> — Cloth only wears to shreds...
> Young ones never hear the death of God
> — Cloth only wears to shreds...

Among the Fang the sun is the symbol of God and it is described overcoming the night:

> With sparking blows of light
> you tear her cloak
> the black cloak lined with fire
> and studded with gleaming stars—

To the Bushmen the moon is the symbol of resurrection:

> You return evermore alive,
> after you vanished from sight.
> Did you not promise us once
> that we too should return
> and be happy again after death?

The Pygmies hail God as the bringer of light:

> He walks along the milky way, he collects the stars.
> With quick arms he piles them into a basket...
> like a woman who collects lizards...

Both the Ewe and the Yoruba sing of the river which the dead have to cross to reach the other world, a motif familiar in classical mythology:

I saw myself carried on a river.
I saw the king of the river and the king of the sun.
There in that country I saw palm trees
So weighed down with fruit,
That the trees bent down under the fruit,
And the fruit killed it.

To the African poet the dead will always remain near to
the living 'like swarming mosquitoes in the evening', and he
expresses the hope that even after death he will be close to
the busy activities of this world:

> Bury me under the great shade trees in the
>     market,
> I want to hear the drums beating
> I want to feel the dancers' feet.

Though death is not the final and absolute separation that
it is in the European concept, the shock of sudden death is
equally great and the Akan poet asks in a beautiful image

> What were your wares
> that they sold out so quickly?

Love finds manifold expression in these traditional poems,
which cover a wide range of emotions, from the Egyptian
poet who compares the delight of seeing his beloved approach
to the pleasure of setting free a trapped bird and seeing it
disappear in the sky, to the down-to-earth Fulani bard who
says of his beloved:

she never stinks of fish,
she never breathes sweat,
like the gatherers of dry wood.

All the poems are of course translations, and the rhythms of African songs are often too complex for English to render them properly. Many African languages are *tonal* languages and the rhythms and sound patterns based on these tonal systems simply have no equivalent in any European language.

One of the most important elements of poetry, however, does survive translation relatively well: the imagery. The originality of the metaphors and images in these poems is a source of constant delight.

God is described as 'resting in the sky like a swarm of bees'. In a terrifying picture it is said of the Yoruba god of war: 'He kills the owner of the house, and paints the hearth with his blood.' And more subtly, but equally terrifyingly, it says of a warrior: 'You kill your opponents gently—like cutting a calabash in half.'

But there is no lack of humour either. Of the very same warrior the poet says: 'Whenever you open your mouth wide, you swallow a hero.' And the Ethiopian bard describes the worthless lover as 'trousers of wind, buttons of hail' or as 'some water in a glass left standing by the fire'. Many of the poets have a wonderful sense of realism and a shrewd observation of details. A Swahili poem about the poor man says:

'The poor man has no manners, he comes along
with the blood of lice under his nails.'

And a Fulani lovesong observes that his beloved's palm is

'sweet to touch like liver'. Even such an unpoetic subject as a colonial European is endowed with striking and beautiful imagery by the African poet:

> His skin is white like salt
> His hair is long like plaited seaweed
> His dress is made of fishes,
> fishes more charming than birds.

I hope that this small volume will help students in Africa towards the study of English poetry and reawaken interest in poetry composed in their African mother tongue. I hope also that it will stimulate interest in many parts of the world outside Africa. For traditional African poetry is not historic; it is not a thing merely to be found in the learned books of social scientists. It is a tradition that is very much alive, which every African schoolchild can study in his own village or town. African poetry has so much vitality that not only does it survive in ritual or traditional social contexts, but it also finds itself new motives and new functions. Anybody who has watched an election campaign in a Nigerian village will know that songs of praise and abuse, composed in the traditional manner, may have more power to swing votes than the speeches of politicians.

U. B.

# RELIGIOUS SONGS

## *Invocation of the Creator*

He is patient, he is not angry.
He sits in silence to pass judgement.
He sees you even when he is not looking.
He stays in a far place—but his eyes are on the town.

He stands by his children and lets them succeed.
He causes them to laugh—and they laugh.
Ohoho—the father of laughter.
His eye is full of joy.
He rests in the sky like a swarm of bees.

Obatala—who turns blood into children.

YORUBA

## The Almighty

Young ones never hear the death of cloth
— Cloth only wears to shreds.
Old ones never hear the death of cloth
— Cloth only wears to shreds.
Young ones never hear the death of God
— Cloth only wears to shreds.
Old ones never hear the death of God
— Cloth only wears to shreds.

YORUBA

## Prayer to the God Thot

The tall palm tree sixty feet high
heavy with fruit:
the fruit contains kernels,
the kernels water.
You who bring water to the remotest place

come and save me because I am humble.
O Thot, you are a sweet well
for him who starves in the desert.
A well that remains closed to the talkative

but opens up to the silent.
When the silent man approaches the well reveals itself;
when the noisy man comes you remain hidden.

EGYPTIAN

## Prayer

Listen to us aged God
listen to us ancient God
who has ears!
Look at us aged God
look at us ancient God
who has eyes!
Receive us aged God
receive us ancient God
who has hands!
If you love beautiful horses take them!
If you love beautiful women take them!
If you love beautiful slaves take them!
Listen to us O God,
O God listen to us.

                              GALLA


## The Creator

The path crosses the river;
the river crosses the path.
Which is the elder?
We made the path and found the river;
the river is from long ago,
from the creator of the universe.

                              AKAN

## The Ancestors

The days have passed;
we are a wandering camp
brighter days before us
perhaps.

Light fades
night becomes darker.
Hunger tomorrow.

God is angry
the elders have gone
Their bones are far
their souls wander.
Where are their souls?

The passing wind
knows it perhaps.

Their bones are far
their souls wander.
Are they far away,
are they quite close?
Do they want sacrifice,
do they want blood?
Are they far,
are they near?

The passing wind
the spirit that whirls the leaf
knows it perhaps.

HOTTENTOT

## Hymn to the Sun

The fearful night sinks
trembling into the depth
before your lightning eye
and the rapid arrows
from your fiery quiver.
With sparking blows of light
you tear her cloak
the black cloak lined with fire
and studded with gleaming stars—
with sparking blows of light
you tear the black cloak.

FANG

## Song for the Sun that Disappeared behind the Rainclouds

The fire darkens, the wood turns black.
The flame extinguishes, misfortune upon us.
God sets out in search of the sun.
The rainbow sparkles in his hand,
the bow of the divine hunter.
He has heard the lamentations of his children.

He walks along the milky way, he collects the stars.
With quick arms he piles them into a basket
piles them up with quick arms
like a woman who collects lizards
and piles them into her pot, piles them up
until the pot overflows with lizards
until the basket overflows with light.

HOTTENTOT

## Prayer to the Moon

Take my face and give me yours!
Take my face, my unhappy face.
Give me your face,
with which you return
when you have died,
when you vanished from sight.
You lie down and return—
Let me reassemble you, because you have joy,
you return evermore alive,
after you vanished from sight.
Did you not promise us once
that we too should return
and be happy again after death?

BUSHMAN

## Hymn to Lightning

In the West the clouds vegetate
in the East they are scattered.
Flowers unfold
white cloud unfolds
mistletoe branches ooze
lightning falls on mistletoe branches
ooze ilbaratree tuffed
killed
weeping
paralysed.
Cruched fire extending
fire having watched fire extending
wood for the fire
bends expands
lightning
beats breaks
water on the surface of clay
where the clouds were together
roaring
continuously
lightning
thundering with spite.

KIJOKU

# DEATH

## *Death*

There is no needle without piercing point.
There is no razor without trenchant blade.
Death comes to us in many forms.

With our feet we walk the goat's earth.
With our hands we touch God's sky.
Some future day in the heat of noon,
I shall be carried shoulder high
through the village of the dead.
When I die, don't bury me under forest trees,
I fear their thorns.
When I die, don't bury me under forest trees.
I fear the dripping water.
Bury me under the great shade trees in the market,
I want to hear the drums beating
I want to feel the dancers' feet.

KUBA

## Prayer before the Dead Body

The gates of the underworld are closed.
Closed are the gates.

The spirits of the dead are thronging together
like swarming mosquitoes in the evening,
like swarming mosquitoes.

Like swarms of mosquitoes dancing in the evening,
When the night has turned black, entirely black,
when the sun has sunk, has sunk below,
when the night has turned black
the mosquitoes are swarming
like whirling leaves
dead leaves in the wind.

Dead leaves in the wind,
they wait for him who will come
for him who will come and will say:
'Come' to the one and 'Go' to the other.
He will say 'Come' to the one and 'Go' to the other
and God will be with his children.
And God will be with his children.

HOTTENTOT

## Lament

Your death has taken me by surprise.
What were your wares
that they sold out so quickly?
When I meet my father, he will hardly recognize me:
He'll find me carrying all I have:
a torn old sleeping mat and a horde of flies.
The night is fast approaching.
The orphan is dying to see its mother.

AKAN


## Lament for the Dead Mother

Mother dear,
Mother you freely give of what you have
fresh food and cooked meals alike.
Mother, listen to me:
the crying child will call after its mother.
Why don't you answer, Mother, when I call?
Are we quarrelling?

EWE

## Funeral Song

Ojea noble Ojea
look around before you depart.
Ojea, behold the fight is over.
Fire has consumed the square,
fire has consumed the house,
Ojea, behold the fight is over.

Ojea, brother Ojea,
ponder and look.
Ojea, behold the fight is over.
If the rain soaks the body,
will the clothes be dry?
Ojea oh, the fight is over.

IBO

## Longing for Death

I have been singing, singing,
I have cried bitterly
I'm on my way.
How large this world!
Let the ferryman bring his boat
on the day of my death.
I'll wave with my left hand,
I'm on my way.
I'm on my way,
the boat of death is rocking near,
I'm on my way,
I who have sung you many songs.

EWE

## Three Friends

I had three friends.
One asked me to sleep on the mat.
One asked me to sleep on the ground.
One asked me to sleep on his breast.
I decided to sleep on his breast.
I saw myself carried on a river.
I saw the king of the river and the king of the sun.
There in that country I saw palm trees
so weighed down with fruit,
that the trees bent under the fruit,
and the fruit killed it.

YORUBA

## Death as a Lotus Flower

I am the pure Lotus,
that blossomed on the horizon,
that grows in the nostril of the sungod.
I am the pure lotus,
that blossomed in the field.

EGYPTIAN

# SORROW

## *Lament*

Listen to my sorrow
listen to my lament.
The bat was struck by misfortune
its head is hanging low.
I too was struck by misfortune
my arms are hanging limp.
The monkey was struck by misfortune
his brothers cease their play.
The lake is full of water
the lake cannot move away.
The room where we are drinking
the room has become dark.
The forest has burst into flames
the hyena looks for its mother.
The antelope flees the forest
the antelope's life is sad.
Listen to my sorrow
listen to my lament.

MAHI

3

## Sadness of Life

The beautiful playing field has fallen to ruins.
The beautiful pleasure ground has fallen to ruins.
Dense forest has reverted to savanna,
our beautiful town has become grassland,
our beautiful home is nothing but grassland.

May the gravedigger not bury me.
Let him bury my feet, let him leave bare my chest,
let my people come and see my face,
let them come and look at my eyes.

The drum does not beat for joy.
'Sadness of Life' 'Sadness of Life' sounds the drum.
The drum only sounds for sadness of life.

EWE

## The Train

The train
carries everybody
everywhere.

It carries the men
it carries the women
it carries me too
a blind boy.
Wherever it carries me
alas, I meet distress
and knock against it
with my knee.
It carries the men
it carries the women,
it carries the blind boy
to his distress.

ITESO

## Loneliness

My wings are plucked—alas!
Must I climb the tree
with hands and feet?
A mother's son is a buttress:
if you have none
down falls the house.
A mother's daughter is
your everyday apparel:
if you have none
you're cold, exposed.
Relations on the father's side
Relations on the mother's side
I have none.
In whom shall I confide?
Oh brother!

EWE

# PRAISE SONGS

## *Praise of Chief Mosenene*

Many-coloured Kraal-snake!
You cross the swelling river
you seek quarrels with Puffadder
the chief who fears war.

Mosenene:
I am a mole, I dig up the earth, I throw up stones;
I rise in the yard of Chief Bullcalf, in order to rob him.

The women:
We kill our children, we bear them for the depth;
the depth of the river will swallow them,
the river will devour them, whose turbulent waters
can only be crossed with sticks.
The child of man says: 'I weep.'
It cuts its skin full of sadness—
O many-coloured Kraal-snake!

SOTHO

## Glory to Moshesh

The herds are saying
We guard these muddy plains
They are saying
We tread deep paths into the fields
Because the earth is dry
The warriors are sweating
The men these real men are dying of thirst
Wiping in vain the sweat
That runs from their brow

The brave Lisiane even
Had to sit down to breathe
He is sitting with Sacroane
Showing no tiredness
Moshesh advances on the city
And reaches the gate through which enter the brave
The women in the houses below
Macheli and Mamachelise
Bend back the reeds
That enclose their huts and say
We want to see
The heifer of many colours
The heifer striped with fire

Macheli and Mamachelise
Say
Let us see the smoke of hot guns
They say
Moshesh is an old toothless leopard
He has torn out his claws
His coat is woven by spiders
His arm is spotted
His shield shines like glowing embers
And he himself like the half moon

They say
Moshesh has seized the white cow
He has shaved her head
He has shorn the heifer Namekoe
They say
The heifer of Moshesh is red and white
His heifers are the fruit of war
Of the war that is won by those who fight valiantly
Let the heifer of Chope enter the town
Amongst cries of grief
And lamentations

They say
an impure serpent has soiled her
The cow of Chopo is no more now than the vulgar beasts
  of the fields
Remove her from the herd lest she defile them
Lead her far away from the town
Let her go and calve among the wild beasts
These herds from where do they come

You may ask Macheli
You may ask Mamacheli
You may ask those who like
To sit on flat rocks near the hills
You may ask those who know how to observe what goes
  on around them

And who talk about it
Ask only those who know from where the booty comes
Ask only those whose wisdom has devised the plan of war
And directed the warriors
Ask the old ones.

SOTHO

## The Timi of Ede

Huge fellow whose body fills an anthill,
You are heavily pregnant with war
All your body except your teeth is black.

No one can prevent the ape
from sitting on the branch of a tree.

No one can dispute the throne with you.
No one can try to fight you.
One who shakes a tree trunk shakes himself.
We do not try to resist you.
The seeds of the Ayo game
do not complain of being shoved about.
You are like death,
who plucks a man's eyeballs suddenly.
You are like a big ripe fruit
that falls on a child at midnight.

Fighting a battle in front
you mark out the next battlefield behind.
My Lord, please give the world some rest.
If one greets you there is trouble;
if one does not greet you there is also trouble.
The fire of destruction is part of your baggage
wherever you go.
You kill your opponents gently,
like cutting a calabash in two.
When the leopard kills,

its tail trails gently on the ground.
Whenever you open your mouth wide,
you swallow a hero.

YORUBA

## The Oba of Benin

He who knows not the Oba
let me show him.
He has mounted the throne,
he has piled a throne upon a throne.
Plentiful as grains of sand on the earth
are those in front of him.
Plentiful as grains of sand on the earth
are those behind him.
There are two thousand people
to fan him.
He who owns you
is among you here.
He who owns you
has piled a throne upon a throne.
He has lived to do it this year;
even so he will live to do it again.

BINI

# WAR

## *War Chant*

The white man has brought his war to the beach.
If they look for bloody battle, they shall have it.
The amazons gather round their king and swear:
With our teeth we shall tear their throats.
Our fire drives them back to the men.
Their priest falls victim to our war.
With their teeth the amazons tore his throat.
Oil palms are felled and come crashing down.
The white man's boat is seized in the lagoon.

FON

## *The God of War*

He kills on the right and destroys on the left.
He kills on the left and destroys on the right.
He kills suddenly in the house and suddenly in the field.
He kills the child with the iron with which it plays.
He kills in silence.
He kills the thief and the owner of the stolen goods.

45

He kills the owner of the slave—and the slave runs away.
He kills the owner of the house—and paints the hearth
    with his blood.
He is the needle that pricks at both ends.
He has water but he washes with blood.

YORUBA

## The Battle of Kadesh

And I, Rameses, spoke to my charioteer;
    Take courage, courage my charioteer
I shall pounce on them like a falcon
I kill them, I slaughter them, I crush them on the earth.
What do these wretches mean to you?
A million of them shall not make me pale.
—And I thrust forward.
Six times I broke through their ranks.
I pursued them like Baal, at the height of his power.
I sowed death and disaster among them.
When my soldiers and charioteers saw
how much I resembled the God of war
in power and in strength
and that my father Amon was with me
and that every country was turned into dust by him,
then they crept closer one by one
and towards evening they advanced towards
the centre of the battlefield
and they saw that the nations I had pounced on
lay torn and bathing in their own blood.

They were the best soldiers of the Hittites,
they were the sons and brothers of their king.
I had left the battlefield of Kadesh white with corpses
One could neither walk nor stand—
the corpses were too many.

EGYPTIAN

# LOVE

## *The Bird Catcher*

I have come to catch birds;
I carry my bird net with me,
a trap in one hand
the net and missile in the other.

Look, all the birds of Punt
are descending on Egypt,
scented with myrrh.
The first bird that lands
fooled by my bait
is fragrant with the perfume of Punt
his claws steeped in balm.

This is my desire:
with you to release it,
to be alone with you
when it sounds the call of freedom,
my bird, scented with myrrh.

I know nothing more beautiful
when I set my traps
than to have you with me.
Glorious: to walk across the field
towards my beloved.

EGYPTIAN

## The Beloved

Diko,
of light skin, of smooth hair and long;
her smell is sweet and gentle
she never stinks of fish
she never breathes sweat
like gatherers of dry wood.
She has no bald patch on her head
like those who carry heavy loads.
Her teeth are white
her eyes are like
those of a new born fawn
that delights in the milk
that flows for the first time
from the antelope's udder.
Neither her heel nor her palm
are rough; but sweet to touch
like liver; or better still
the fluffy down of kapok.

FULANI

## Love Song

I painted my eyes with black antimony
I girded myself with amulets.

I will satisfy my desire,
you my slender boy.
I walk behind the wall.
I have covered my bosom.
I shall knead coloured clay
I shall paint the house of my friend,
O my slender boy.
I shall take my piece of silver
I will buy silk.
I will gird myself with amulets
I will satisfy my desire
the horn of antimony in my hand,
Oh my slender boy!

BAGIRMI


## Love Song

The body perishes, the heart stays young.
The platter wears away with serving food.
No log retains its bark when old,
No lover peaceful while the rival weeps.

ZULU

## The Negligent Lover

That which flows is water,
but that which scoops—what is it?
That which flows is tears,
but that which moves me, what is it?

That which rains is God,
but the cloud is only a shadow.
That which cries is the heart,
but the tears are only a shadow.

The goose is happy,
because it does not drown.
You are like God,
whose heart knows no desire.

GALLA


## The Worthless Lover

Trousers of wind and buttons of hail;
A lump of Shoa earth, at Gondar nothing left;
A hyena bearing meat, led on a leather thong;
Some water in a glass left standing by the fire;
A measure of water thrown on the hearth;
A horse of mist and a swollen ford;
Useless for anything, useful to no one;
Why am I in love with such a man as he?

AMHARA

## Excuses

Are you leaving me because you are hungry?
What! Are you the slave of your stomach?

Are you leaving me to cover yourself?
Haven't I got a blanket on my bed?

Are you leaving me because you are thirsty?
Then take my breast.

It flows over for you.
Blessed the day of our meeting.

EGYPTIAN

# PEOPLE

## *The Poor Man*

The poor man knows not how to eat with the rich man.
When they eat fish, he eats the head.

Invite a poor man and he rushes in
licking his lips and upsetting the plates.

The poor man has no manners, he comes along
with the blood of lice under his nails.

The face of the poor man is lined
from the hunger and thirst in his belly.

Poverty is no state for any mortal man.
It makes him a beast to be fed on grass.

Poverty is unjust. If it befalls a man,
though he is nobly born, he has no power with God.

SWAHILI

## The European

In the blue palace of the deep ocean
dwells a strange being.
His skin is white like salt
his hair is long like plaited seaweed.
His dress is made of fishes,
fishes more charming than birds.
His house is built of brass rods
his garden is a forest of tobacco leaves.
His country is strewn with white pearls
like sand on the beach.

CAMMA

## The Irresponsible Student

If you only knew
the horror that is wine
you would curse it.
They taught you to sing to the flute
they taught you to lament to the shepherd's reed;
they taught you to recite to the harp
they taught you to sing praises to the zither.

You sit in the bar
sit between harlots;
you want to be aggressive.

You sit between the girls
steeped in fragrant ointment
a wreath of flowers round your neck—
you are drumming on your belly.

You sway, you fall on your face,
you are covered in dirt.

EGYPTIAN

## The Lazy Man

When the cock crows,
the lazy man smacks his lips and says:
So it is daylight again, is it?
And before he turns over heavily,
before he even stretches himself,
before he even yawns—
the farmer has reached the farm,
the water carriers arrived at the river,
the spinners are spinning their cotton,
the weaver works on his cloth,
and the fire blazes in the blacksmith's hut.

The lazy one knows where the soup is sweet
he goes from house to house.
If there is no sacrifice today,
his breastbone will stick out!

But when he sees the free yam,
he starts to unbutton his shirt,
he moves close to the celebrant.

Yet his troubles are not few.
When his wives reach puberty,
rich men will help him to marry them.

YORUBA

# ANIMALS

## *The Magnificent Bull*

My bull is white like the silver fish in the river
white like the shimmering crane bird on the river bank
white like fresh milk!
His roar is like the thunder to the Turkish
    cannon on the steep shore.
My bull is dark like the raincloud in the storm.
He is like summer and winter.
Half of him is dark like the storm cloud,
half of him is light like sunshine.
His back shines like the morning star.
His brow is red like the beak of the Hornbill.
His forehead is like a flag, calling the people from a distance,
He resembles the rainbow.

I will water him at the river,
With my spear I shall drive my enemies.
Let them water their herds at the well;
the river belongs to me and my bull.
Drink, my bull, from the river; I am here
to guard you with my spear.

DINKA

59

## Song of the Lioness for her Cub

Fear the one
who has sharp weapons
who wears a tassel of leopard tail,
he who has white dogs—
O son of the short-haired lioness!
My short-eared child,
son of the lioness who devours raw flesh,
you flesh-eater!
Son of the lioness whose nostrils are red with
     the bleeding prey,
you with the bloodred nostrils!
Son of the lioness who drinks water from the swamp,
You water-drinker!

HOTTENTOT


## Kob Antelope

A creature to pet and spoil
An animal with a smooth neck.
You live in the bush without getting lean.
You are plump like a newly-wedded wife.
You have more brass rings round your neck
than any woman.

When you run you spread fine dust
like a butterfly shaking its wings.
You are beautiful like carved wood.
Your eyes are gentle like a dove's.
Your neck seems long, long
to the covetous eyes of the hunter.

YORUBA

## Colobus Monkey

We ask him to come and die—he sulks.
He dies at last—his cheeks are full of laughter.
Two rows of neat white teeth.
Death always follows war.
Those who wake early must sweep the ground.
Colobus says: the eagle sweeps the sky;
let me sweep the top of the tree.
Abuse me—and I will follow you home.
Praise me—and I will stay away from you.
Colobus is a friend of the man in rags,
and a friend of the man in the embroidered gown.
He kills lice with black nails.
Deep-set eyes.
A mighty tail.
Don't hold my tail,
don't play with my face.
Death always follows war.

YORUBA

## Viper

The viper lives in the forest.
Not even the Ogun worshipper can pick it up.
Viper's child is beautiful in its nest.
But *Nini* is the most beautiful of snakes.
It is better for Nini to change its colour
and go home and bring some colour for Viper.
Viper owns all the rats in the forest.
Viper owns all the bush in the forest.
Viper owns all the snakes in the forest.
If there is no rat, what will snake eat?
If there is no rat, it will eat mouse;
if there is no mouse it will eat a shrew.
Poisonous death,
Poisonous viper,
Beautiful viper.

YORUBA

# CHILDREN'S SONGS

## *Lullaby*

Someone would like to have you for her child
but you are mine.
Someone would like to rear you on a costly mat
but you are mine.
Someone would like to place you on a camel blanket
but you are mine.
I have you to rear on a torn old mat.
Someone would like to have you as her child
but you are mine.

AKAN

## *Song*

Europeans are little children.
At the river bank they shot an elephant.
Its blood became a canoe, and it sank;
and it sank oars and all.
I collected wild sorghum for Miss Mary.

NYASA

## The Sun

Where are your children, sun?
Where are your children?
As you have eaten all your own
why do you chase the moon
to take her children for your own?
You can never succeed—
go and look for your own.

EWE

## The Sky

The sky at night is like a big city
where beasts and men abound,
but never once has anyone
killed a fowl or a goat,
and no bear has ever killed a prey.
There are no accidents; there are no losses.
Everything knows its way.

EWE

## A Baby is a European

A baby is a European
*he does not eat our food:*
he drinks from his own water pot.

A baby is a European
*he does not speak our tongue:*
he is cross when the mother understands him not.

A baby is a European
*he cares very little for others;*
he forces his will upon his parents.

A baby is a European
*he is always very sensitive:*
the slightest scratch on his skin results in an ulcer.

EWE

## Song

Mother Mother shave me
let us go and see the bird
with the bright red beak.
Let's go to the bush Mother
to the small bush.
Let's brush off our hair
each other's hair.
Let us leave a guide-bone
for the goats that graze
that graze in my little field.
The little field I cultivate
I cultivate with a hoe
I bought in the European's home
the home where moss grows.
We shall bring forth a child
and we shall name him
and we shall name him *darkness*.

NYASA

## The Moon

The moon lights the earth
it lights the earth but still
the night must remain the night.
The night cannot be like the day.
The moon cannot dry our washing.
Just like a woman cannot be a man
just like black can never be white.

SOUSSOU

## The Sweetest Thing

There is in this world something
that surpasses all other things
in sweetness.
It is sweeter than honey
it is sweeter than salt
it is sweeter than sugar
it is sweeter than all
existing things.
This thing is sleep.
When you are conquered by sleep
nothing can ever prevent you
nothing can stop you from sleeping.
When you are conquered by sleep
and numerous millions arrive
millions arrive to disturb you
millions will find you asleep.

SOUSSOU

## The Well

There is a well
that has five kinds of water.
There is sugared water
and salty water.
There is tasteless water
and bitter water.
The fifth water is red
red like blood.
This well is the head.

SOUSSOU

# NOTES ON THE POEMS

INVOCATION OF THE CREATOR, p. 17
*Ohoho*: the sound of laughter.
*Obatala*: name of the Yoruba creator god. It is said that he not only created human beings at the beginning, but that he forms *every child* in the womb, before it is born. Hence 'he turns blood into children'.

PRAYER TO THE GOD THOT, p. 18
*Thot* (often spelt Thoth): the Egyptian god of wisdom.
In a country where the greatest natural threat is drought, water is the symbol of life and of God himself.

THE CREATOR, p. 19
This is an invocation used by Akan drummers when they want to refer to God's creative power and antiquity.

THE ANCESTORS, p. 20
The Mbuti are pygmies. They have been driven by more powerful tribes into the Ituri forest, where they live a wandering life, founding no permanent setlements. As they cannot stay in one place they cannot look after the tombs of their ancestors, and so the wind, which moves everywhere, has to them become a symbol of the spirits of the dead.

HYMN TO THE SUN, p. 22
In the literature of many nations the sun is visualized as a hunter or warrior who rises every day in the east to fight and conquer the night.

SONG FOR THE SUN THAT DISAPPEARED BEHIND
THE RAINCLOUDS, p. 22

This song expresses the idea that though the sun may disappear
or 'die' God will always recreate it, and that he will always
bring back light into the world.

PRAYER TO THE MOON, p. 23

The moon is here used as a symbol of resurrection and eternal
life. As the moon dies and is born again, so men also want to
have a new life after death.

HYMN TO LIGHTNING, p. 24

This poem does not address lightning—it tries to convey the
impression of the sudden, jerky power of lightning and of the
confusion it causes in a thunderstorm. That is why the rhythm
of the poem is deliberately jerky and the sequence of images is
deliberately disorderly.

DEATH, p. 25

The poet here gives expression to the idea that the dead are not
completely separated from the living. They want to hear the
drums beating, they want to feel the dancers' feet—because they
still want to take some part in the affairs of the living.

PRAYER BEFORE THE DEAD BODY, p. 26

Such a gloomy vision of life after death is rare in Africa, where
usually it is assumed that death does not create a complete and
final break with the living. The poetry of pygmies and bushmen,
though, often conveys a similar feeling of hopelessness.

LONGING FOR DEATH, p. 30

Like the Yoruba, the ancient Greeks and many other people,
the Ewe believe that the dead have to cross a dark river in order
to reach the next world.

### THREE FRIENDS, p. 31

Once again the crossing of a river is used as the symbol of death. The palm tree that is weighed down and killed by its own fruit is like an old man who is survived by many children.

### DEATH AS A LOTUS FLOWER, p. 31

This is a strange poem in which death does not appear as something frightening or terrifying but as something absolutely perfect and beautiful. Death, in other words, is seen as the perfect conclusion to life and perhaps the opening of the gate to a higher form of existence.

### PRAISE OF CHIEF MOSENENE, p. 37

A terrifying poem in praise of a warrior king who is subtle and dangerous like a snake. The women, in praising the king, say that they bear their children for death—that their sons are merely destined to die in the army of Mosenene.

### GLORY TO MOSHESH, p. 39

This poem is in praise of another powerful Sotho chief. Although we hear of a battle and the conquest of a town, this is not a narrative poem giving a sequence of events. Various images are drawn: of tired warriors; of frightened but admiring women watching the entry of Moshesh into the city; of a defiled white heifer, who is drawn out of the city, and who could stand for the honour of the tribe or of the women who were raped. Numerous images are used to describe the glory of Moshesh: he is called a 'heifer striped with fire', his coat is 'woven by spiders' and he shines 'like the half moon'.

### THE TIMI OF EDE, p. 42

The Timi of Ede was a general of the King of Oyo who was sent to defend the king's frontier. He built the frontier town of Ede and later installed himself there as a semi-independent king.

In typical Yoruba fashion the king is praised with a mixture of awe and humour. Some of the images are terrifying ('You kill your opponents gently, like cutting a calabash in two') but others are intended to be humorous: 'Whenever you open your mouth wide, you swallow a hero.'

WAR CHANT, p. 45

The Fon people in Dahomey carried on prolonged wars against the French, until they were finally conquered in 1894. This song relates to an actual event when the Dahomean warriors captured a boat of Whydah and killed a French priest.

*Amazons:* women soldiers. The king of Dahomey was said to have three thousand wives in his palace; most of them were made to fight in the army in times of war.

THE BATTLE OF KADESH, p. 46

This poem in praise of Rameses the Second, one of the most famous of the Egyptian Pharaohs, is written as if Rameses himself were speaking. He is telling the story of his victory over the Hittites at Kadesh. The Hittites established an empire in what is now Turkey and expanded south into modern Syria, where they clashed with the Egyptians at the town of Kadesh, on the River Orontes.

*charioteer:* many ancient peoples of the Middle East fought in light, two-wheeled, open carriages drawn by swift horses. The horses were controlled by the driver, called a charioteer; the warrior in the chariot thus had both hands free for fighting.

*Baal:* a God of the Canaanites, one of the peoples living in Palestine at the time of Rameses II.

*Amon:* worshipped by Egyptians under Rameses II as the most powerful of all the Gods.

THE BIRD CATCHER, p. 49

*missile:* a throwing-stick or perhaps a dart.

*Punt*: the name given by the ancient Egyptians to Eastern Africa, probably including most of modern Somalia. From Punt the Egyptians obtained gold and incense.

*myrrh*: the gum yielded by the incense tree, which grew in Eastern Africa and Arabia. It comes through the bark from inside, and smells fragrant.

*claws steeped in balm*: the idea is that the bird has perched on an incense tree where myrrh has gathered on the bark, and carried this perfumed substance on its claws all the way to Egypt.

### THE BELOVED, p. 50

*fawn*: the young of an antelope or deer.

*udder*: the bag of milk under a cow or antelope.

*the fluffy down of kapok*: kapok is a soft, cotton-like material that comes from the seeds of a tropical tree.

### LOVE SONG, p. 51

*Antimony*: a metal that is ground and used to paint the eyelids.

### THE NEGLIGENT LOVER, p. 52

A song of sorrow about unrequited love. The lover appears as remote as God and as little in need of affection as God himself.

### THE WORTHLESS LOVER, p. 52

*Shoa*: a central province in Ethiopia.

*Gondar*: an ancient capital of Ethiopia.

*thong*: strap.

### THE IRRESPONSIBLE STUDENT, p. 56

*reed*: an instrument like a flute, but cut from reed.

*harp*: an instrument in the shape of a bow with strings to pluck.

*zither*: an instrument with strings over a sounding-board. They are plucked or strummed.

*steeped*: soaked.

THE MAGNIFICENT BULL, p. 59

The Turks controlled Egypt for centuries. The Egyptians may have used Turkish cannon when they later gained control over the Sudan.

SONG OF THE LIONESS FOR HER CUB, p. 60

*Tassel of leopard skin*: part of the hunter's dress—a long piece of leopard skin hanging from his cap or his back.

KOB ANTELOPE, p. 60

*Brass rings*: white markings on the antelope's neck.

COLOBUS MONKEY, p. 61

*His cheeks are full of laughter*: the dead monkey has his teeth bared, as if he was laughing.
*Let me sweep the top of the trees*: allusion to the bushy, broom-like tail of the Colobus.

VIPER, p. 62

*The Ogun worshipper*: worshippers of Ogun, the Yoruba god of war, sometimes walk about with a python round the neck. But not even they could handle a viper.
*Shrew*: a mouselike animal that has a strong smell.

SONG ('Europeans are little children'), p. 63

This song expresses the bewilderment of the child at the purposelessness of the behaviour of Europeans.

SONG ('Mother Mother shave me'), p. 66

This is the type of improvised song which children often sing when they put everything that comes to their mind to a tune. The poem has no logical sequence and no story. Its mood is carefree and lighthearted.

# SOURCES OF THE POEMS

INVOCATION OF THE CREATOR, p. 17: collected and translated by Ulli Beier.

THE ALMIGHTY, p. 18: from *Olodumare*, by Dr B. Idowu.

PRAYER TO THE GOD THOT, p. 18: from *Der Blinde Harfner*, by Bertus Aafjes.

PRAYER, p. 19: from *Galla Verskunst*, by Enno Littmann.

THE CREATOR, p. 19: Kwabena Nketia, in *Black Orpheus*, 3.

THE ANCESTORS, p. 20: from *Les Pygmes de la Grande Sylve Ouest Equatoriale*, by P. Trilles.

HYMN TO THE SUN, p. 22: from *Le Totemism chez les Fang*, by P. Trilles.

SONG FOR THE SUN THAT DISAPPEARED BEHIND THE RAINCLOUDS, p. 22: from *Les Pygmes de la Grande Sylve Ouest Equatoriale*, by P. Trilles.

PRAYER TO THE MOON, p. 23: from W. Schmidt, *Ursprung der Gottesidee*.

HYMN TO LIGHTNING, p. 24: Miriam Koshland, in *Black Orpheus*, 2.

DEATH, p. 25: from *Jeune Afrique*.

PRAYER BEFORE THE DEAD BODY, p. 26: from *Les Pygmes de la Grande Sylve Ouest Equatoriale* by P. Trilles.

LAMENT, p. 28: Kwabena Nketia, in *Black Orpheus*, 4.

LAMENT FOR THE DEAD MOTHER, p. 28: Geormbeeyi Adali Mortty, in *Black Orpheus*, 4.

FUNERAL SONG, p. 29: Chief Dennis Osadebay, in *African Affairs*.

LONGING FOR DEATH, p. 30: from *Das Alte und das Neue Lied im Ewelande*, by P. Wiegrabe.

THREE FRIENDS, p. 31: from *Yoruba Poetry*, by Bakare Gbadamosi and Ulli Beier.

DEATH AS A LOTUS FLOWER, p. 31: from *Der Blinde Harfner*, by Bertus Aafjes.

LAMENT, p. 32: collected and translated by Ulli Beier.

SADNESS OF LIFE, p. 34: from *Grammatik der Ewe Sprache,* by D. Westermann.

THE TRAIN, p. 35: Gerhard Kubik, verbal communication.

LONELINESS, p. 36: Geormbeeyi Adali Mortty, in *Black Orpheus,* 4.

PRAISE OF CHIEF MOSENENE, p. 37: from *Versuch Einer Grammatik der Sotho,* by Karl Endemann.

GLORY TO MOSHESH, p. 39: from *African Songs,* by Leon Damas.

THE TIMI OF EDE, p. 42: collected and translated by Ulli Beier.

THE OBA OF BENIN, p. 43: John Bradbury, in *Nigeria Magazine.*

WAR CHANT, p. 45: M. Clement da Cruz, verbal communication.

THE GOD OF WAR, p. 45: from *Yoruba Poetry,* by Bakare Gbadamosi and Ulli Beier.

THE BATTLE OF KADESH, p. 46: from *Der Blinde Harfner,* by Bertus Aafjes.

THE BIRD CATCHER, p. 49: from *Der Blinde Harfner,* by Bertus Aafjes.

THE BELOVED, p. 50: Malam Hampate Ba, in *Présence Africaine.*

LOVE SONG, p. 51: from *Essai de Grammaire de la Langue Baguirmienne,* by H. Gaden.

LOVE SONG, p. 51: from *Darkness and Light,* by Peggy Rutherfoord.

THE NEGLIGENT LOVER, p. 52: from *Ethnographie Nord-Ost Afrikas.*

THE WORTHLESS LOVER, p. 52: from *Darkness and Light,* by Peggy Rutherfoord.

EXCUSES, p. 53: from *Der Blinde Harfner,* by Bertus Aafjes.

THE POOR MAN, p. 55: from *Swahili Poetry,* by L. Harries.

THE EUROPEAN, p. 56: from *Savage Africa,* by W. W. Reade.

THE IRRESPONSIBLE STUDENT, p. 56: from *Der Blinde Harfner,* by Bertus Aafjes.

THE LAZY MAN, p. 57: from *Yoruba Poetry,* by Bakare Gbadamosi and Ulli Beier.

THE MAGNIFICENT BULL, p. 59: Cummins, in *Journal of the Anthropological Institute*, 1904.

SONG OF THE LIONESS FOR HER CUB, p.60: Thomas Hahn, in *Globus*, 1867.

KOB ANTELOPE, p. 60: Bakare Gbadamosi and Ulli Beier, in *Odu*, 9.

COLOBUS MONKEY, p. 61: Bakare Gbadamosi and Ulli Beier, in *Odu*, 9.

VIPER, p. 62: Bakare Gbadamosi and Ulli Beier, in *Odu*, 9.

LULLABY, p. 63: Kwabena Nketia, in *Black Orpheus*, 3.

SONG, p. 63: from *African Affairs*.

THE SUN, p. 64: Kafu Hoh, in *Voices of Ghana*.

THE SKY, p. 64: Kafu Hoh, in *Voices of Ghana*.

A BABY IS A EUROPEAN, p. 64: Kafu Hoh, in *Voices of Ghana*.

SONG, p. 66: from *African Affairs*.

THE MOON, p. 68: from *Etudes Guinéennes*, 1 (1947).

THE SWEETEST THING, p. 68: from *Etudes Guinéennes*, 1 (1947).

THE WELL, p. 69: from *Etudes Guinéennes*, 1 (1947).

# INDEX OF FIRST LINES